©OHYOURESOTOUGH, 2022
ALL RIGHTS RESERVED

NO PART OF THIS BOOK MAY BE REPRODUCED OR TRANSMITTED IN ANY FORM OR BY ANY MEANS, ELECTRONIC OR MECHANICAL, INCLUDING PHOTOCOPYING AND RECORDING, OR BY ANY INFORMATION STORAGE AND RETRIEVAL SYSTEM, WITHOUT PERMISSION IN WRITING FROM THE AUTHOR CHELSEY GOMEZ.

This book is dedicated to my magical and beautiful daughter Luna.

ADHD is Magic!

written and illustrated by Chelsey Gomez

The Tale of a Little Witch Named Bea Who Has ADHD

Hi I'm Bea and I'm a witch who has ADHD!

Having ADHD isn't always easy or fun.

I always felt a little different from everyone.

MY ADHD MADE it HARD to PAY attention in SCHOOL.

"BEA, ARE YOU LISTENING?"

UNFORTUNATELY MY TEACHERS DIDN'T THINK THAT WAS VERY COOL.

I could never sit still.

"Just chill!"

Jumping around doing cartwheels was much more of a thrill!

One day I realized my ADHD wasn't tragic... It's actually the source of all of my magic!

So let me tell you how...

ADHD has made me into the amazing person I am now!

HOCUS POCUS HELP ME FOCUS!

ADHD HELPS ME THINK OUTSIDE OF THE BOX!

Good Job!

BEING CREATIVE TOTALLY ROCKS!

ADHD GIVES ME ENERGY!

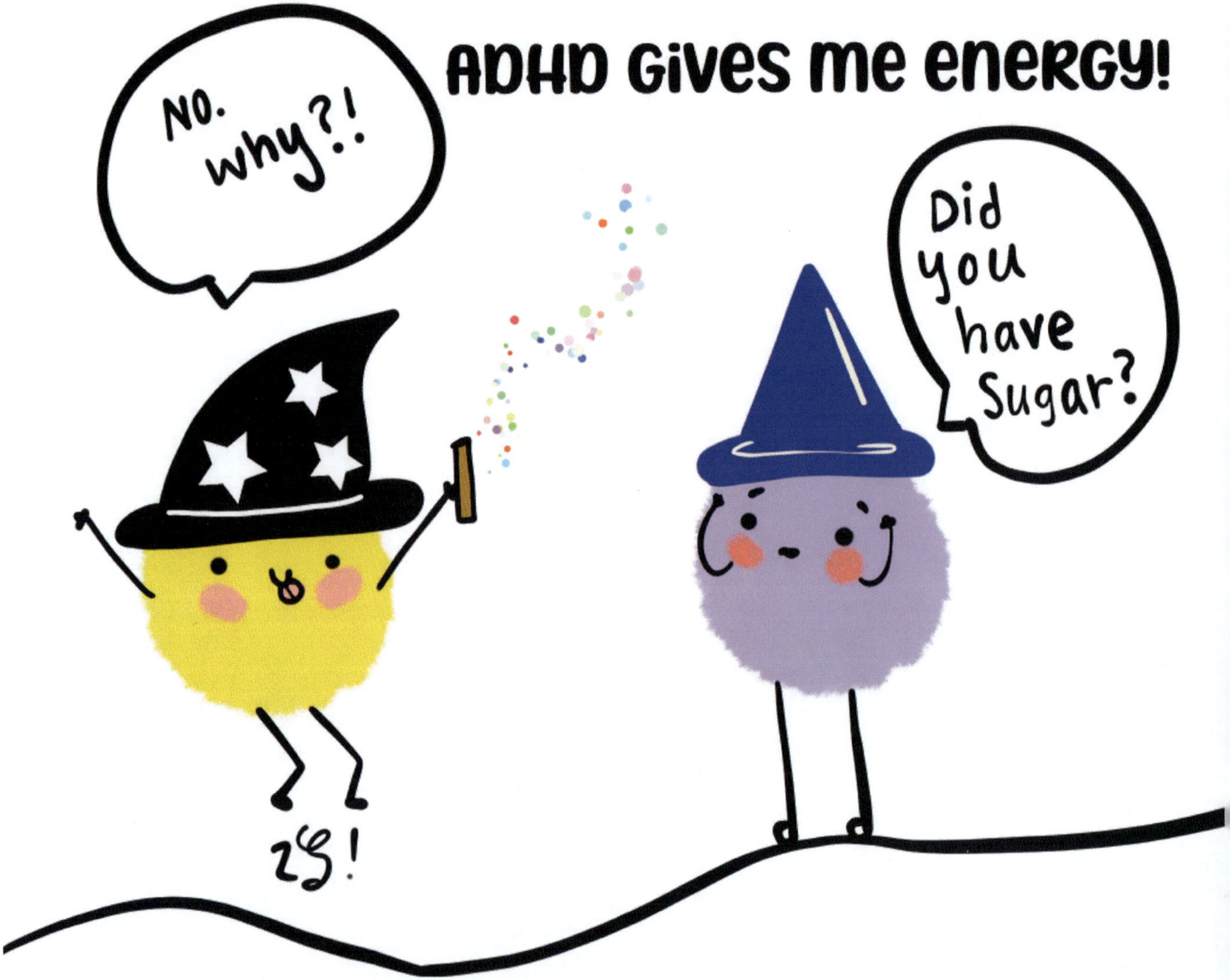

I DON'T EVEN HAVE TO DRINK COFFEE!

ADHD MAKES SOLVING PROBLEMS EASY.

ABRACADABRA LEMON SQUEEZY!

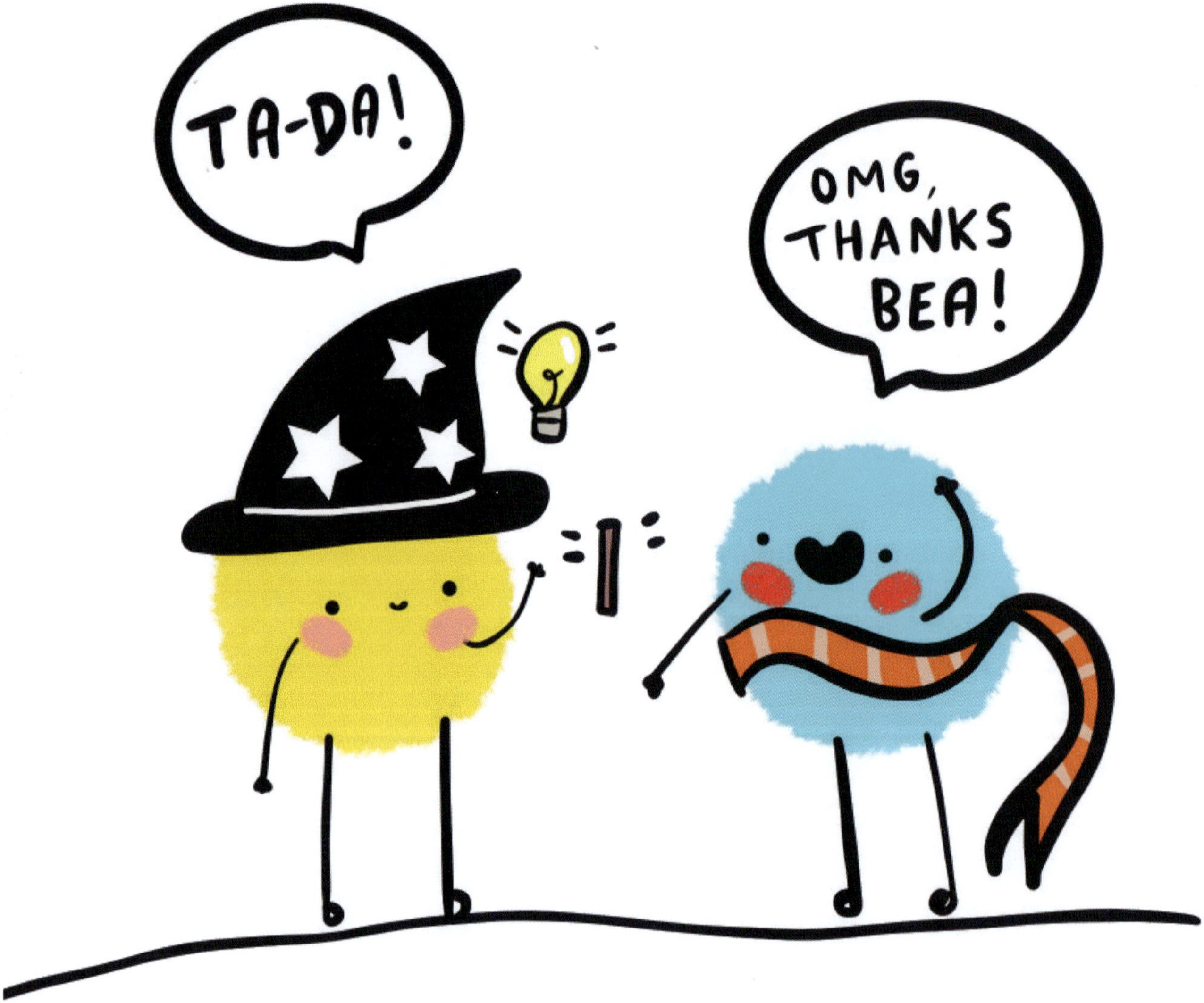
TA-DA!
OMG, THANKS BEA!

My ADHD helps me be funny!

"What's a ghost's favorite treat?"

"Ice-scream!"

"HAHA HA!"

Now I wish I had some ice scream in my tummy!

I CAN FOCUS ON THINGS I LOVE QUITE WELL.

FOCUS!

FOR ME, THAT'S CASTING A SPELL!

ADHD HELPS ME BE A GOOD FRIEND.

B.F.F.S

on me... you can always depend!

ADHD HELPS ME KEEP CALM IF I'M NOT PERFECT.

I'LL KEEP PRACTICING UNTIL I GET IT CORRECT!

ADHD HAS TAUGHT ME TO BE FAIR.

Let's split it!

Yum cookie!

I ALWAYS HELP OTHERS AND I KNOW HOW TO SHARE!

I am smart, kind, funny, creative, and more!

"HI"

ADHD

My ADHD has helped me realize there's a lot about me to adore!

ADHD is a part of who I am and that's okay!

It makes me special and I like it that way!

So next time your ADHD makes you feel blue...

Remember just how special it makes you too!

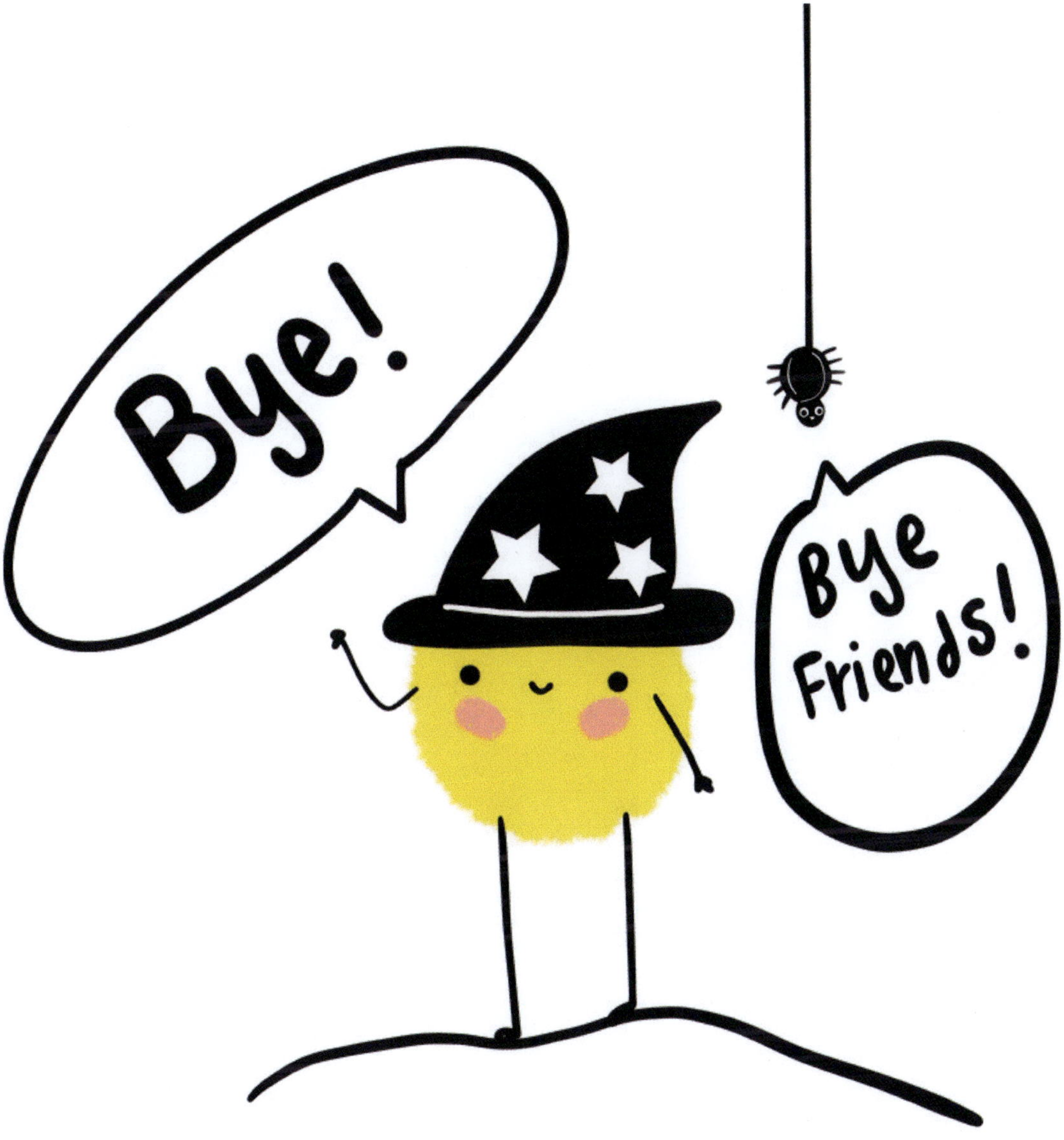
Bye!
Bye Friends!

Printed in Great Britain
by Amazon